IMAGES
of America

THE ROAD TO
HUNTING ISLAND
SOUTH CAROLINA

Prior to the opening of the Beaufort River Bridge in 1927, the only means of transportation between Beaufort and the other sea islands was by ferry or private boat. This form of travel could be a dangerous proposition when heavy weather and/or thick fog shrouded the river. The bridge's opening marked the beginning of a road construction project that would eventually link most of the sea and barrier islands with Beaufort. (Courtesy of Beaufort Museum.)

IMAGES
of America

THE ROAD TO
HUNTING
ISLAND
SOUTH CAROLINA

Nathan Cole

ARCADIA

First published 1997
Copyright © Nathan Cole, 1997

ISBN 0-7524-0823-2

Published by Arcadia Publishing,
an imprint of Tempus Publishing, Inc.
2 Cumberland Street, Charleston SC 29401.
Printed in Great Britain

Library of Congress Cataloging-in-Publication Data applied for

*To the memory of my mother and father, Alberta and Finis Cole,
who never visited the island
and to my wife and daughter, Kathy and Amanda,
who love the island as much as I do.*

Contents

Acknowledgments 6

Introduction 7

1. The Planters 9

2. Frogmore 27

3. The Shrimpers 45

4. Hunting Island State Park 55

5. The Wildlife Sanctuary 91

6. A Vanishing Paradise 111

Acknowledgments

A special thanks to Jerry Morris for his editorial assistance.

Thanks also to the South Carolina Department of Archives and History, the Duke University Special Collections Library, Melinda Smyre, Alcoa South Carolina Inc., The Beaufort County Library, The Beaufort Museum, Gay Seafood Company, Sally Carr, and all those who searched their family photo albums for images of Hunting Island.

Introduction

Hunting Island is a barrier island located 16 miles southeast of Beaufort, South Carolina. The island received its name during the Colonial period due to its use as a hunting preserve by the planters of the area. It has been called South Carolina's best known secret because an estimated one million people currently visit the state park each year, yet very little advertising is done to actively promote tourism to the island. People who visit the island probably received their information by suggestions from friends and relatives. The 5,000-acre island with its 4-mile stretch of beach can sometimes become congested, but the people who visit the island are a breed apart from the standard beach tourist. They are not seeking tee-shirt shops and fancy restaurants, nor do oceanfront condominiums and wall-to-wall bodies sunning on the beach impress them. As one visitor remarked, "If I had wanted to go to a circus, I would have gone to the Grand Strand." A guest at Hunting Island is seeking more than gaudy trinkets and sculpted golf courses. He or she is trying to find the solitude and solace of a natural paradise at an affordable price. They want to relax during their vacation, not after it.

Hunting Island does not have a history of use as either a permanent residential area or as farmland because of its size, topography, and difficulty of access. The plantation owners of the eighteenth and nineteenth centuries established it as a recreational area and that application of the island's resources has continued until the present. It could be said that there are, in actuality, two Hunting Islands residing in the same location. The first island is a wildlife sanctuary with a semi-tropical climate, protective barrier dunes, maritime forests, and a broad spectrum of wildlife. The second island is a vacation destination used by people from all of the continental forty-eight United States. Each island has its own unique qualities which are separate yet interlocked, for the island impacts the people as much as the people impact the island.

A road is a means by which a destination is reached. Since Hunting Island was never developed for permanent human habitation, people traveled distinctly different roads to reach the island. The Beaufort area was first visited by the Spanish in 1566 where they established a settlement called Santa Elena on what is now Parris Island. The second oldest city in South Carolina, Beaufort was established in 1711 by the plantation barons who made their fortunes growing indigo, rice, and cotton on the surrounding islands. As men of leisure, these planters would mount week-long expeditions to the island to hunt deer, small game, and water fowl. The black slaves who were imported to work the planter's fields caught shrimp, crabs, and fin fish in the water around the island, which was used to prepare meals for their families that were reflections of their African heritage. Fripp Inlet, at the southern end of the island, served as a connector between the inland rivers and open ocean for the pirates, fishermen, and other mariners who made their living on the sea. Today, a guest at Hunting Island State Park can fish, take walks on trails or along the beach, collect shells, or simply sit and watch the clouds frolic with the ocean waves.

The island itself has traveled many roads to its present condition. Originally a part of several islands collectively known as the "Hunting Islands," the land later became known as Reynolds' Island because it was owned by the Reynolds Family from the early 1700s until the occupation by Union soldiers during the War Between the States. In 1859, the United States government acquired a tract of land on the island in order to erect a lighthouse for use as an aid in navigation. When a group of sea island planters purchased the southern end of the island for use as a hunting preserve, Reynolds' Island became Hunting Island. When the War Between the States began, Beaufort was one of the first cities targeted for capture by Federal forces. The plantation owners fled inland, "abandoning" their homes and property which were later sold at auction for "back taxes."

By the 1920s, Hunting Island was owned by the U.S. government and two private absentee landlords. A local movement was begun to persuade the owners to donate the land to Beaufort County for the creation of a public park and game sanctuary. After the lighthouse was taken out of service in 1933, the county gained full ownership of the property from the other two owners. Financial pressures created by the Great Depression forced the county to transfer title of the island to the state of South Carolina, and in 1938, Hunting Island became a state park. Thus, the land was saved from commercial and residential development which would have excluded a large segment of the population from the enjoyment of the island's beauty.

Hunting Island is my spiritual home, my "One Particular Harbor." It has been a place of refuge during times of adversity in my life, and it was where I went to recuperate following a serious illness. However, because of the dynamics of a barrier island, Hunting Island is in a constant state of change. All barrier islands are transient land, continuously being reshaped and relocated by the very forces which created them. A high rate of natural beach erosion is causing Hunting Island to disappear. Every trip to the island is a reminder that, as my beard grows grayer, we both are slowly fading away.

On the neighboring barrier islands, the time has arrived when people are now selling sea breezes and sunrises while landmovers cover the past. My desire is to leave a vision of Hunting Island to future generations when there is nothing left to see. This was a difficult project because there is no comprehensive collection of historic photographs available. Most of the planters had their records, pictures, and other documents confiscated or destroyed by Union troops. The island was privately held until the 1930s and was only used by selected individuals who were not interested in keeping records. Photographers for the Civilian Conservation Corps visually recorded the work they were doing during the island's transition to a park, but the majority of photographs made of Hunting Island are scattered in scrapbooks in Georgia, South Carolina, New York, and the other states from where visitors came to the island.

When I am on the island, I try to be up and on the beach before the sun rises. The combination of clouds, surf, and light is like a gigantic kaleidoscope, and this unique mixture creates some of the most beautiful scenes on the island. The prismatic effect of the atmosphere give the sun's rays a range of colors that is almost like the essence of life. One particular morning, the sun was dancing on the clouds, making the sea oats appear as if they were made of golden fire. I began to set up my 4x5 camera to record the image when a man and wife, who had been taking an early morning walk on the beach, stopped to watch what I was doing. They asked several questions, and when I had the camera ready to make the exposure, I offered to let them see what was on the viewing screen. The man didn't say much, but his wife told me, "I have been coming to the island for years and have passed by this place many times, but this is the first time I have really seen it. Thank you for showing it to me."

Nathan Cole
April 1997

One
The Planters

This drawing shows an indigo plant from which was produced a brilliant blue dye. Sometimes called the "Devil's Dye" because of its connections with slavery, the dye satisfied a British craze for East Indian exotica. It became the most important cash crop of the Port Royal Island plantations and brought immense wealth to the planters. The British markets for indigo disappeared when the United States gained its independence from England. (Courtesy of Duke University Special Collections Library.)

The town of Beaufort was located on a high bluff which overlooked a river. It was founded in 1711 on Port Royal Island to stop the northward expansion of the Spanish and to act as a port for the planters to export the agricultural products from the sea island plantations. The settlement was named after Henry Somerset, the Duke of Beaufort and one of the Lords Proprietors. In the 1690s, the Lords Proprietors of Carolina began to issue land grants to planters, the majority of whom came from Barbados. These vast areas of rich land in Carolina began to produce great quantities of valuable agricultural products. On the sea islands of Port Royal and St. Elena, rice was cultivated, but due to problems associated with flooding the fields, the crop did not attain the importance it did in the Charles Towne-Georgetown areas. (Courtesy of Beaufort County Library.)

The Cultbert House on Bay Street is an example of the many magnificent summer homes built in Beaufort by the planters. Edgar Fripp, a member of the largest family on the sea islands, built "Tidalholm," Paul Hamilton named his residence "The Oaks," and Robert Barnwell created his "Castle." Collectively, these houses, along with the great wealth they represented, made South Carolina's second oldest town the "most aristocratic" city in the South until the War Between the States. (Courtesy of Beaufort County Library.)

The sons of the sea island planters were expected to be educated gentlemen, able to move easily in international trading circles. Beaufort College was chartered in 1795 by influential citizens of Beaufort to prepare their young men before sending them to Harvard, Yale, or to England to complete their education. The college was eventually integrated into the University of South Carolina system.

Religion was an important part of the planter's spiritual and social life, and the Episcopal church was the church of the planter class. St. Helena's Parish was founded in 1712, and the church building was constructed in 1724. The brick structure is coated with a layer of pink stucco, and its interior is elaborately finished with shutters, columns, and an upper gallery. (Courtesy of Beaufort County Library.)

The names of the elite planter families are etched in the tombstones of St. Helena's church cemetery. "Tuscarora Jack" Barnwell is buried here, along with members of the Fripp, Sams, Elliot, and Coffin families. During the War Between the States, the flat, marble gravestones were used by Union doctors as operating tables to treat soldiers injured in the re-taking of Port Royal Harbor.

Beaufort is the traditional starting point on the road to Hunting Island. Renamed the Robert Woods Memorial Bridge, this gateway to the sea and barrier islands is now included as part of U.S. Highway 21. The Beaufort River is part of the intercostal waterway, thus the structure is capable of swinging open to allow tall vessels to pass. Travelers have to be patient, for when the bridge is open, road traffic can back-up for several miles and be stalled for lengthy periods of time. Once across the river, one passes through Ladys Island to St. Helena's Island, the sea island where the great plantations were located.

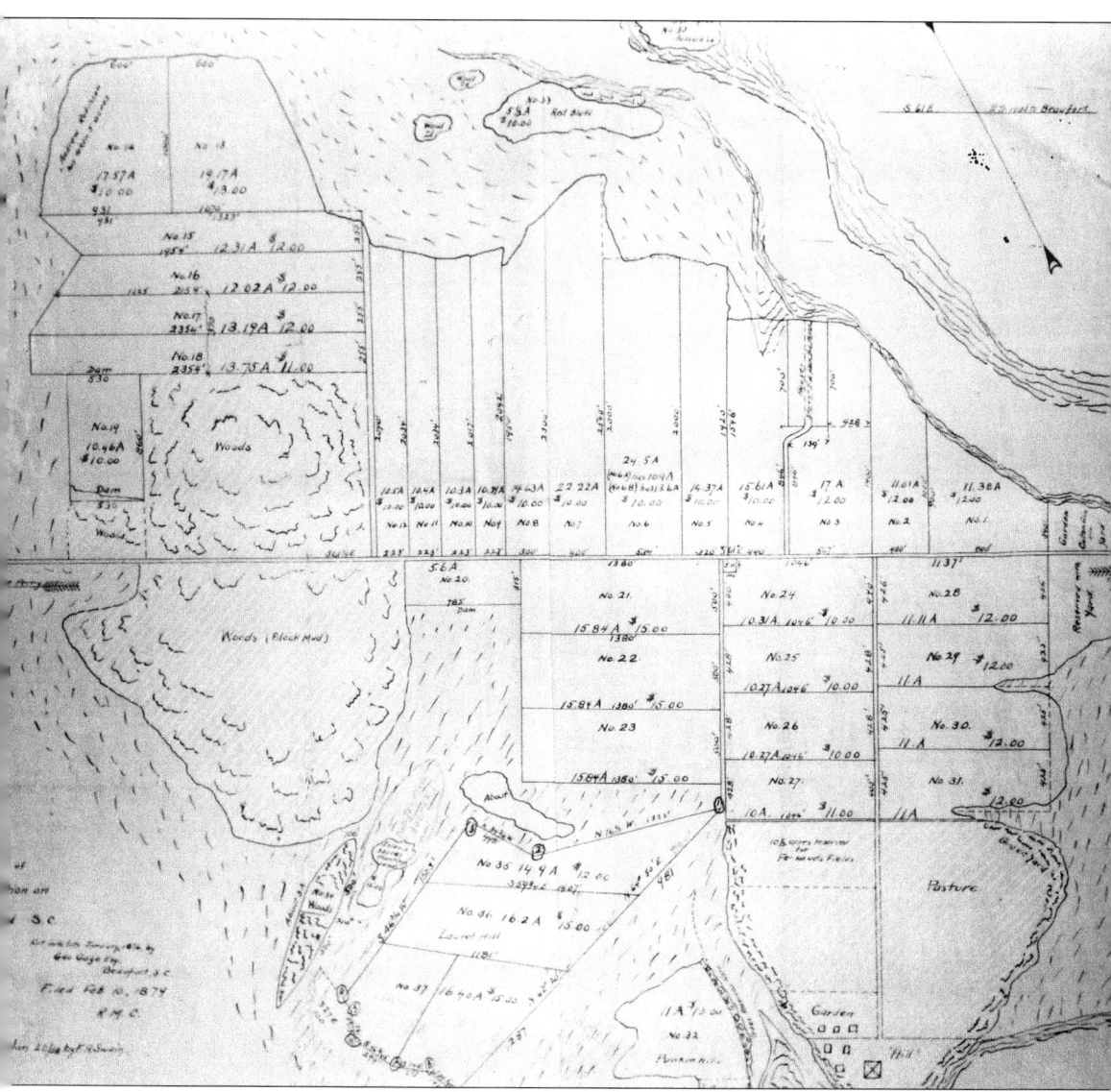

The most visible symbol of a planter's wealth was land, as shown by this drawing of the Eustis Plantation. The planters invested money and labor in large tracts of land to produce an agricultural crop. This product of the plantation was then sold by dealers to the industrialized areas of the Northern states and foreign countries. The plantation system was, in effect, the most efficient and specialized Southern enterprise of its era. Wealth brought notice and influence, and the planters became important forces in the forging of a national economy through the production of the bulk of the nation's staple crops. As generations passed, the planters emulated their British counterparts and eventually achieved the status of landed aristocracy, which was the closest the United States would come to having a titled nobility. (Courtesy of Beaufort County Library.)

The operation of a sea island plantation more closely resembled the West Indies plantations than those of the inland Southern counterparts. The planter was not involved in daily operations. Instead, he would hire an overseer to whom he would communicate the jobs to be performed. The overseer selected drivers, usually trusted slaves, who were responsible for getting the work accomplished. As this drawing of indigo production shows, work was divided into "tasks" and a time limit was assigned for the completion of each task. Thus, there was a separation between the "master's" time and the "slave's" time, and if the slave completed his tasks ahead of schedule, the remainder of the task time belonged to the slave. This "task" system of operation allowed the sea island planters to become gentlemen of leisure who could devote their time to the military, government service, the professions of law and medicine, and scientific projects. (Courtesy of Duke University Special Collections Library.)

When the United States gained its independence from England, the market for indigo disappeared. The cash crop which replaced indigo was long stapled, sea island cotton. The quality of this variety of cotton was so high that dealers could demand and receive twice the market price of upland cotton. Sea island cotton ushered in the "Golden Age" of the planters and generated much more wealth than had indigo. (Courtesy of the collection of Melinda Smyre.)

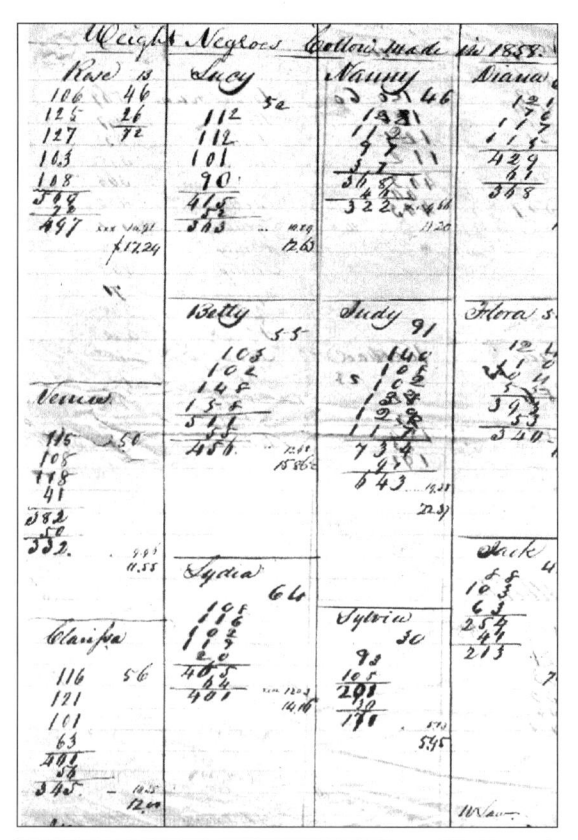

Most planters were meticulous in keeping detailed records of all the activities that occurred on the plantation. This tally sheet show the weight of cotton picked by each field hand on a daily basis. Knowing how much weight was picked helped place a cash value on both the plantation and the slave. The slave's worth was important in case of sale or the leasing of a slave's labor to other planters.

The rivers which bisected the islands could be used to sail a freighter directly to a planter's dock. If the captain knew the location of the shoals and other hidden obstacles at high tide, he could take his vessel up the waterway to the dock. The cotton was loaded while the tide was low; then at the next high tide, the ship could head for the open sea. (Courtesy of South Carolina Archives and History.)

A plantation was both an agricultural enterprise and a home, with each having its own name and story. By 1790, most sea island planters maintained two or more houses. One was on or near the actual plantation and the other was located in Beaufort or some other inland city. The planter would stay at the island house from November to May and then move inland to escape the mosquitoes and the deadly "country fever," or malaria. One of the more notable plantation compounds was Datha. The island was purchased after the Revolutionary War by William Sams and was continuously owned by the Sams family until the beginning of the War Between the States. William Sams was one of the first planters to introduce sea island cotton to the St. Helena area.

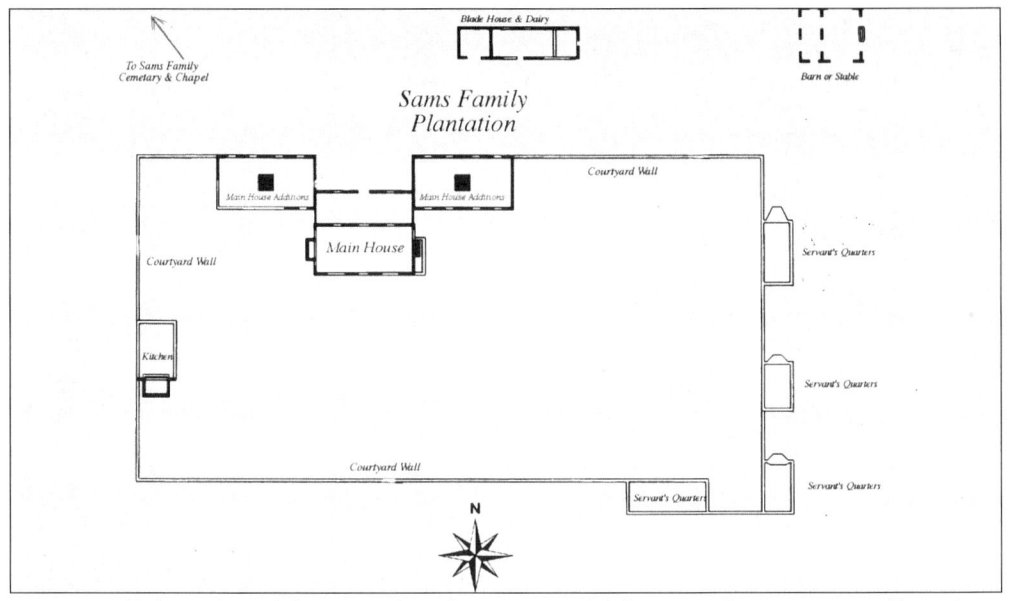

Ruins are all that is left of the original Datha compound following a fire in 1876. William Sams had built the center portion of the main house, and his son, Barnwell, added the two wing additions after William's death. The land was declared "abandoned" and, by executive order, set aside to be auctioned off for taxes to the former slaves who had worked there. (Courtesy of Alcoa South Carolina, Inc.)

All the buildings and walls in the compound were constructed from tabby, a building material that was introduced to the area by the Spanish. Oyster shells are burned to obtain lime; the lime is mixed with sand and oyster shells and then poured into molds to form walls and roofs. The finished building is very sturdy, energy efficient, and has a subtle pinkish color that is unique to tabby.

It was from these sea island homes that the planters would mount week-long expeditions, at times accompanied by their family and slaves, to Hunting Island. The taking of deer, ducks, and other small game was not only a sport for the planter but served a practical purpose. While vegetables could be grown in gardens for food, these hunting trips were a major source of meat for the families on the plantations. A group of planters eventually purchased the southern end of Hunting Island for use as a private preserve.

The sea island plantations were so secluded that it could take over a half day's travel to reach Beaufort. This meant that the families had to be almost totally self-sufficient, even in the area of religion. Datha had its own chapel a short distance from the main house where the family could meet to singularly worship or to receive the sacraments from priests who made irregular visits from St. Helena's parish. (Courtesy of Beaufort County Library.)

Attached to Datha's chapel was the family cemetery. Most of those buried at Datha are children, for childhood was the most dangerous period in a person's life due to disease and the island environment. A giant live oak tree spread its limbs over the graves like a protective angel, keeping all who resided there safe from any further harm. (Courtesy of Beaufort County Library.)

The "Golden Age" of the planters ended with the War Between the States, yet most of the plantations remained intact and undamaged due to the early Union occupation. This photograph of the Robert Fuller plantation, made in the spring of 1865, has a note on the back that reads, "Rob. Fuller plantation dwelling house on St. Helena Island. 5 miles from Beaufort on Wallace Creek. Now owned by E.S. Philbrick, Esq. & managed by T.E. Ruggles. T.E.R. & his sister are seen in this picture. This is a very pretty & cozy place. It is where I stayed in Sept. 1865 while keeping store for E.S.P." This is an unusual photograph, for very few historical documents about the planters remain. Union occupation troops seized the planter's personal and business records and shipped them north. Some planters transferred their memorabilia inland to Barnwell, Orangeburg, and Columbia, only to have them burned by Sherman's army. (Courtesy of Beaufort County Library.)

Contrary to government claims, the planters never "abandoned" their fields. The land is still used for large-scale planting of agricultural crops. This field has been primed and is waiting to be planted, not in cotton, but in tomatoes. The raised beds have been covered with a protective plastic, and buried in the soil are pipe lines which consistently deliver the correct amount of water and nutrients to the plants.

Thousands of tomatoes will grow in one field, and each plant will require a stake set in the ground to support the plant. While the fields are designed to require little maintenance, some manual labor is still required to set the stakes and pick the fruit. In the past, these "tasks" would have been performed by slaves, but now Hispanic migrant workers provide the labor.

The original system of marketing the crop remains intact. This is just one of several large packing houses located on St. Helena Island. While the packing house owners have their own fields of tomatoes to process, they also act as dealers for other producers in the area. The tomatoes are delivered in large wooden boxes to the houses where they are graded, culled, packaged, and shipped nationwide. In 1991, tomatoes were the top cash crop for South Carolina with $55.5 million in sales. Beaufort County ranked second in the state in the production of farm products. From May to well into July, trucks loaded with tomatoes and bound for Northern markets add to the congestion of traffic on the Sea Island Parkway.

Two
Frogmore

As the title of ownership indicates, the negative aspect of the plantation system was slavery. The Barbados planters were given vast areas of crop land but were faced with an acute labor shortage. Yet, less than 10 percent of the black slaves imported into the New World came to North America, and those who were brought to the sea island plantations were considered skilled labor.

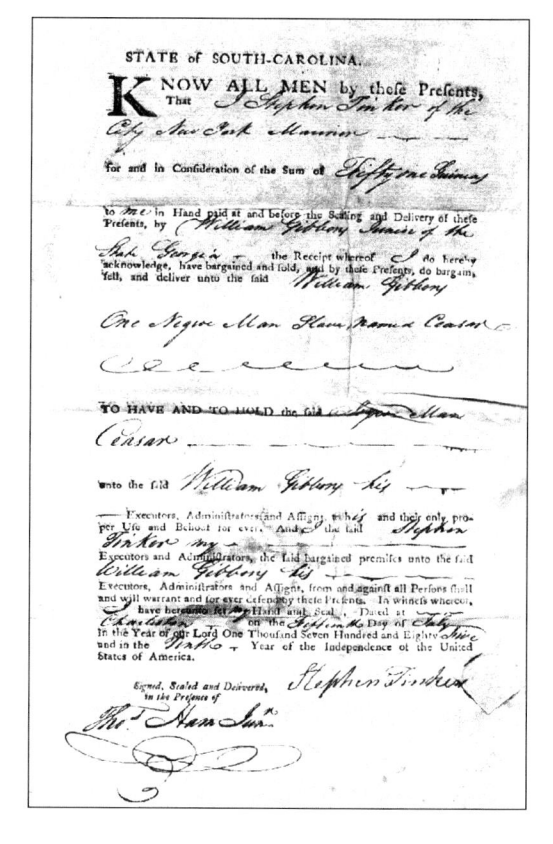

The use of slaves was legal in the United States until the passage of the Thirteenth Amendment to the U.S. Constitution in 1865. The practice of slavery was not isolated entirely to the South as slaves were also used in the Northern states. The practice of slavery dates back to mankind's early history and was an accepted institution in all known civilizations. A Southern slave could cost $2,000, equal to the price of a tractor in 1990s dollars. If nothing else, most planters wanted to protect their investments, for a dead slave had no value.

Life as a slave was hard. Work was performed in high, humid heat, and there was barely enough food to stay alive. Pneumonia was the most common cause of death among slaves. Because the slaves outnumbered the whites, the master's greatest fear was slave rebellion, so strict laws were enacted to curtail any thoughts or plans of revolt. Incredibly, as undesirable as these conditions were, they were better than the fate of a South American slave; there, the sugar plantations and mines were deathtraps that killed more than a million slaves because the owners considered the blacks a dispensable part of production. (Courtesy of Beaufort County Library.)

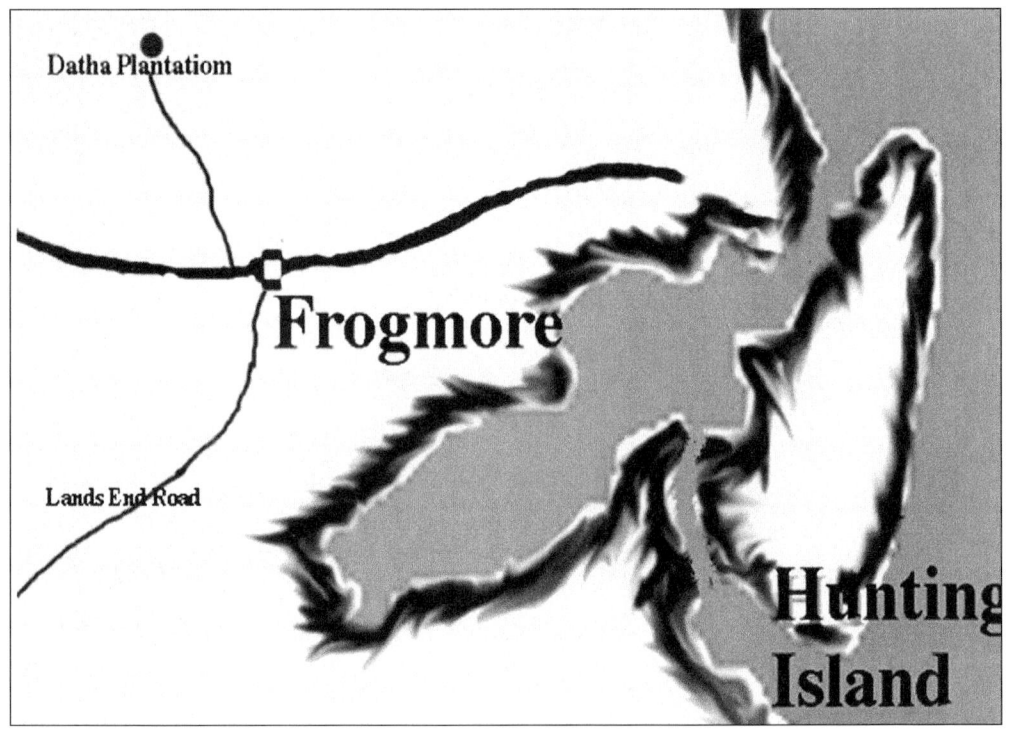

As communities go, Frogmore appears to be rather insignificant. A look at the map shows that Frogmore is important because it is the crossroad where the the Beaufort-St. Helena Road connects with the Datha Island Road and Lands End Road. Along these tributary roads lay a large portion of the plantation lands, and the planters used these "highways" for access to the seaport in Beaufort.

When the Union troops captured the Beaufort area, the plantation slaves were set free. Roles became reversed when the slaves became masters of the land where they had once been forced to work. These events helped form one of the largest black communities in the Low Country. Most of the present businesses which operate in Frogmore are involved in keeping alive the Gullah traditions of the former slaves.

Approximately thirty plantations had frontage on Lands End Road by the beginning of the War Between the States. Sometimes called the Old White Church, the Chapel of Ease was also situated on the road. It was built about 1740 as an extension of St. Helena's Parish to provide a place for the planters to worship without having to travel to Beaufort.

The Chapel of Ease is considered to be one of the finest remaining tabby structures left in the Low Country. After the American Revolution, the chapel was separated from St. Helena's Parish to form a separate church. The building burned in a forest fire in 1886 and was never restored. The ruins were used in a quick shot in the movie *The Big Chill*, which was made during the 1980s.

Thomas Jefferson felt that slavery should not have been allowed in the new nation, but he also wrote that slaves should not be freed when they possessed little education and few skills. After the jubilation of being freed from their masters, the former slaves had to face the realization that they now had to provide for themselves. While a small percentage were skilled artisans, most had been uneducated field hands. The Penn School was established in Frogmore on Lands End Road by missionaries from the Northern Benevolent Societies. They used education and economic independence to help the freedmen become U.S. citizens. In 1905, the school incorporated Booker T. Washington's method of industrial instruction, thus broadening the scope of the school's curriculum. Recently, the Penn Center has been assisting black landowners whose land titles are in doubt from having their land taken by land developers. Using a method called "partition sales," these developers acquire from the black landowners large tracts of land where they can then build expensive homes and golf courses.

The planters heavily impacted the lives of the slaves, but in very subtle ways, the blacks also influenced the lives of the planters. At first, the planters tried to use Native American slaves in the fields, but they were too susceptible to European diseases and too hard to locate when they escaped. The planters tried to use indentured servants. However, the available servants were few in number and, being of European origin, were also subject to malaria. The planters' early reluctance to use black slaves was overcome by the Lords Proprietors, several of whom were slave traders. They gave incentives of extra land to planters who owned slaves. Black slaves were more desirable because of their genetic resistance to malaria and their ability to work in a semi-tropical climate. Of course, the slaves were not empty vessels, ready to absorb English culture when they arrived in the New World. Instead, they brought with them their strong African traditions and culture, which were blended with experiences from the West Indies and life on the sea island plantations to form a creole lifestyle which became known as Gullah.

De Good Nyews Bout Jedus Christ Wa Luke Write

Luke

Luke Tell Theophilus Wa Dis Book Taak Bout

Chapter 1

1 ¹ Deah Theophilus, plenty people beena try fa write down all de ting wa we beliebe fa true, wa done happen mongst us. ² An all wa dey done write down, dis de same ting wa de people dem dat been wid Jedus wen e fus staat, dey done tell we. An dey beena preach God Wod. ³ So, Honarable Theophilus, A figga since A done beena study bout dem ting good fashion from de time dey fus staat, A oughta write um down fa you step by step from staat ta finish. ⁴ A da write fa make you kno all de trut consaanin dem ting wa dey done laan you, fa leh you kno dat all dis wa dey laan you bout done happen fa true.

De Angel Tell Zechariah E Gwine Habe Son

⁵ Same time wen Herod been king ob Judea, one Jew priest nyame Zechariah been dey. E been one ob de priest dem ob Abijah group. An e wife nyame been Lizabet. Lizabet blongst ta de fambly ob

1 Forasmuch as many have taken in hand to set forth in order a declaration of those things which are most surely believed among us,

2 Even as they delivered them unto us, which from the beginning were eyewitnesses, and ministers of the word;

3 It seemed good to me also, having had perfect understanding of all things from the very first, to write unto thee in order, most excellent Theophilus,

4 That thou mightest know the certainty of those things, wherein thou hast been instructed.

5 There was in the days of Herod, the king of Judaea, a certain priest named Zacharias, of the course of Abia: and his wife *was* of the daughters of Aaron, and her name *was* Elisabeth.

The most tangible expression of the Gullah lifestyle is the language. Long suppressed as a corrupted form of English, Gullah is now believed by scholars to be as distinctive a dialect as can be found in secluded areas of the Appalachian Mountains. *De Good Nyews Bout Jedus Christ Wa Luke Write* (1995) is one of the first published attempts to put into writing a language which has been spoken for centuries by black sea islanders. (Courtesy of The American Bible Society, New York.)

Frogmore Stew

2 Tabls. olive oil	1 large onion
1 bunch fresh parsley	1 clove of garlic
1 stalk of celery	1 bell pepper
2 Tabls. Old Bay Seasoning	1 bay leaf

3 lbs. of smoked sausage cut in 2" lengths
2 lbs. of small potatoes
8 ears of fresh corn cut in 2" lengths
4 lbs. of shrimp, still in shell
3 Tabls. of red pepper hot sauce.

Chop the pepper, onion, garlic parsley and celery. Heat large frying pan and add oil. Saute vegetables with sausage & seasonings. In a large pot, boil the potatoes in a gallon of water & hot sauce until tender.

Combine the sausage and vegetable mixture with the potatoes & water. Add the corn & boil 5 minutes. Add the shrimp & simmer until the shrimp turn pink.

Serve with hot corn bread.

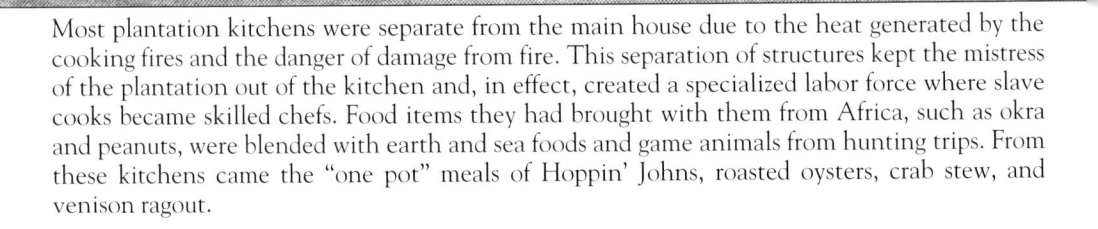

Most plantation kitchens were separate from the main house due to the heat generated by the cooking fires and the danger of damage from fire. This separation of structures kept the mistress of the plantation out of the kitchen and, in effect, created a specialized labor force where slave cooks became skilled chefs. Food items they had brought with them from Africa, such as okra and peanuts, were blended with earth and sea foods and game animals from hunting trips. From these kitchens came the "one pot" meals of Hoppin' Johns, roasted oysters, crab stew, and venison ragout.

The art of basket-making was also brought from Africa. Baskets were in great demand on the plantations for storing food, harvesting crops, and providing extra income from sales at the market. Baskets made of sweet grass were particularly prized in the main house for storing bread, fruits, clothes, and other household items. Their fragrance of fresh hay added a unique quality to their utility. Basket-making is still being practiced, but is in decline. There are few people willing to learn the discipline to weave the baskets, and land developers have cut off a majority of access to the major sources of sweet grass plants and the roadside locations used to market the product.

One Gullah tradition brought from Africa lived underground on the plantations. This was their religious belief in evil spirits and the magic of root medicine to cure or kill. This faith in the supernatural mixed with Christian dogma to form a hybrid religion. Root doctors were forbidden to practice their craft by the planters in fear that they would be poisoned. Yet, the practice has continued to the present, and Frogmore is considered to be one of the most powerful voodoo centers in America. The acceptance of spiritualism is so great that a past High Sheriff of Beaufort County was also a practicing root doctor because he often had to remove spells and curses before he could perform his legal duties. St. Helena is also where the famous root doctor, Dr. Buzzard, is buried. This belief in the supernatural is best exemplified by the story of the Graybeards.

Spanish moss is a non-parasitic plant that grows on the branches of trees. It gathers nourishment and water from atmospheric humidity and air borne dust. The Low Country trees abound with the plants which hang like pendants from the trees. In areas where the trees have overgrown the roadways, they form eerie, web-like tunnels.

Spring comes early to the sea islands, and the story goes that a young truck driver was delivering a load of agricultural supplies to a plantation near Lands End. He had been to Beaufort before, but this was his first trip to the sea island farms. His route to the storage barns took him down a tree-lined, sandy road. The sun was just rising, and he watched in his mirrors as the light played on the moss as it rustled in the breeze created by the truck.

As a work gang unloaded the truck, an old black man with white hair checked off the items on the manifest. In an effort to communicate, the driver mentioned to the checker how beautiful the moss had appeared in the early morning light. The old man appeared to be shocked and began rapidly talking to the driver in what he later learned was Gullah. The driver managed to get the old man to slow down so he could understand what was being said.

The old man told the driver that the moss was the sign that the tree was haunted by the spirit of a Graybeard. The Graybeards were the souls of evil planters and slaves alike who, after death, had been trapped forever inside the tree to do penance for their sins. The spirit still retained the ability to grow hair and the moss was the beard of the spirit.

The old gentleman claimed the trapped souls were always restless and seeking revenge because of their fate. They would take out their anger by suddenly dropping branches on a man's head to kill him or by being blown over during a storm to destroy a house. At night, he said, when the breezes came from the ocean and across the marshes, the low moans of their voices could be heard, lamenting their fortune.

The driver was awed at the old man's words, for he obviously believed very deeply in the Graybeard spirits. When the unloading was finished, the driver got silently back in his truck to return to his warehouse. As he made his way back down the tree-lined road, the beauty he had seen was replaced with a more sinister vision. He would make many more trips to the sea islands, and during quiet moments when he passed under moss-draped trees, he wondered what one had to have done to become a Graybeard.

The Frogmore Frog stands mutely at the entrance to the old post office in Frogmore. There is no record of when or who placed the cement statue there. Local residents say that it has been there for as long as they could remember. Recently, the U.S. Postal Service tried to change the name of Frogmore by building a new post office building and naming it St. Helena. Hopefully, their attempt to change a name on a map will be in vain. As long as someone remembers to tell the stories of other South Carolina towns that were eliminated by the federal government, such as Dunbarton and Ellington, then Frogmore will always live on.

Three
The Shrimpers

Fishing for shell and fin fish in the waters surrounding Hunting Island has been done since the time the Native Americans occupied the area. The commercial harvesting of shrimp began in the late 1800s. Shrimp has become the most valuable fishery in the United States, with Americans consuming 1 billion pounds of the shellfish annually. While the largest producers of wild-caught shrimp are in the Gulf of Mexico, a large segment of the citizens of Beaufort County rely on shrimp for their livelihood. (Courtesy of Beaufort County Museum.)

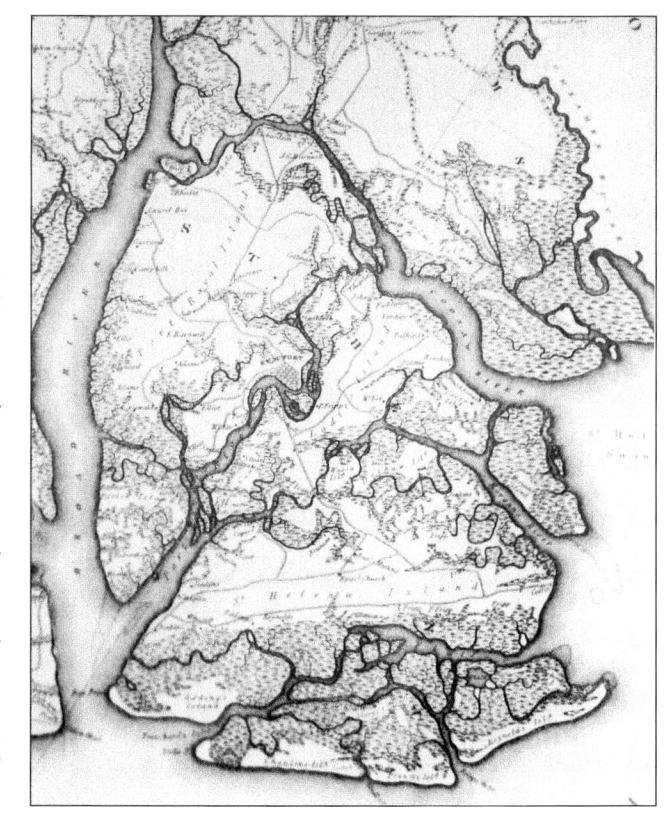

The first shrimpers used small, shallow draft boats similar to this one to pull long seine nets in the shallow rivers and shoal waters. The development of improved trawls or nets allowed the boats to work deeper waters. Pressure to increase production to meet higher demand led to larger boats with greater working ranges. (Courtesy of Gay Seafood Company.)

Though the boats differ in length and style, they are usually standardized in their method of fishing. Most use a twin trawl system which tows four nets. The nets are about 40 feet wide at the mouth. Two to three people are required to operate the boat. The captain stays at the wheel, especially in shoal waters, while one or two strikers work the nets.

Like a flotilla of warships, a group of shrimp boats troll the ocean waters as the sun rises over Hunting Island. The best time to catch shrimp is between midnight and dawn, so the boats leave the docks very early in the morning to be on station when the shrimp start running. Shrimping is an industry that is heavily influenced by tradition. The boats are mostly owner-operated, family-run enterprises. The shrimpers value their independence and are not very open to strangers. Most of the present-day shrimpers are the children of shrimpers, and there is a strong comradery among individual shrimping families. Superstition also plays a part in their lives. When a shrimper buys a boat, he will rarely change her name because of the bad luck it could bring. Most shrimpers cannot imagine themselves in any other form of employment. As one captain said, "Once you get marsh mud between your toes, you can't leave it."

Little Amber spreads her nets even in the middle of a summer squall. When the shrimp are running, only the most severe weather will keep a boat at the dock. The captain and the strikers are paid according to the poundage of shrimp caught. When eight to ten hours of work yield only 40 pounds of shrimp, both the striker and the captain have lost money.

Though the boat heads back to the dock, the work continues. The strikers must finish heading and grading the shrimp, clean the fin fish which can be sold, and dispose the bycatch or "trash" fish. There is always a flock of birds around the incoming boat to eat the waste being thrown overboard.

A shrimp boat returns to the dock from the ocean via the network of rivers and creeks that wind their way through the tidal marshes. Some of the boat owners have private docks at their homes, but most shrimpers tie up at the market where they will sell their catch. There the boats will stay until it is time to sail again.

When driving toward Hunting Island, one can sometimes see what appears to be boats docked in the middle of a grassy field, but the boats are actually floating in a tidal creek that is hidden by marsh grass. This is the dock of Gay's Seafood Company, located at the southern end of St. Helena. The company was started in 1948 by Captain "Buster" Gay and is now operated by his sons.

Among the most expensive items on the shrimp boat are the trawls. These nets can cost upwards of $3,000. The cost is increased by federally required Turtle Escape Devices (TEDs), which help stop endangered sea turtles from being drowned, and Bycatch Release Devices (BRD units) used to reduce the amount of bycatch and death of larger game fish.

The winch is a very important device on the boats. It controls the booms that deploy and retrieve the trawls. A heavy net filled with shell and fin fish would be difficult for a man to handle even with pulleys. A single man on the winch can retrieve the heavy nets and swing them around to be dumped in the sorting box. (Courtesy of Gay's Seafood Company.)

When the nets are positioned over the sorting box, the bottom is opened and the collected sea creatures are dumped. The shrimp are graded, headed, and placed into baskets for icing down. Fin fish and large crabs to be sold are separated. Unusable fish, such as stingrays and sharks, are sent down the chute and dumped back into the water. (Courtesy of Gay's Seafood Company.)

The gloves lying on a shelf are the symbol that another work day has ended. Hunting Island is important for the shrimpers, and the shrimp are important to the visitors to Hunting Island. Stops at a local produce stand for fresh corn, okra, and melons and then at a fish market for a couple of pounds of fresh shrimp provide the ingredients for a hungry camper to prepare a "Low Country Boil."

The life of a shrimper is sometimes nomadic. The captain has to follow the shrimp and their seasons to make money. Pink shrimp are found in Florida waters while white shrimp live off the Georgia-South Carolina shores. Brown shrimp can be found along the North and South Carolina coast. A Federal Management Plan governs the Atlantic fishery and provides for seasons and closure, if needed, to protect stocks.

Miss Tiffany belonged to Captain Robert Gay. When it was found that worms had invaded the hull and the cost of repair would have been greater than buying another boat, all essential machinery was removed, and she was beached. Miss Tiffany is symbolic of the problems the shrimpers are facing. Reduced catches, more regulation, and higher operating costs have cut into profits. The year 1996 was considered by St. Helena shrimpers to be the worst year in their memory, but hope sustains their culture with the belief that the next season will be better.

Four
Hunting Island State Park

Hunting Island continued to be a prime hunting area into the twentieth century. This 1927 promotional publication extols the virtues of the barrier islands of the Low Country to wealthy Northerners as sites for hunting and fishing.

At the end of the 1920s, a group of local citizens began a movement to make Hunting Island into a county park. Once the three different owners had donated the land to Beaufort County in the mid-1930s, the work began. A major part of the process of transforming the island was constructing a means of motorized access to the island. The St. Helena road ended at the edge of the marshes near the Harbor River. Causeways had to be built across the salt marshes, and bridges had to be erected over the Harbor River and Johnson's Creek. This costly project would have been impossible during the years of the Great Depression without the assistance of the Civilian Conservation Corps (CCC). This New Deal Program was started to help ease the country's financial difficulties, and in the process, the CCC built seventeen state parks in South Carolina alone.

The construction of the causeways began in the late 1930s, and it was a tough, dirty job. Work schedules were governed by the tides, and the workmen had to endure oppressive heat, humidity, and mosquitoes. There were no nearby quarries or other sources of landfill, so material had to be dug out of the marsh mud. Yet, despite the adversities, the "civilian soldiers" engineered roadways that are still currently used. (Courtesy of Beaufort Museum.)

This photograph of the causeway was made in July 1939 and shows the progress of the road. The causeways were the most important part of the project because stable platforms had to be in place before bridge abutments could be set. (Courtesy of Beaufort Museum.)

The men who worked in the marshes were called "mud puppies." There was no heavy land moving equipment available to transport material, so the most common tool used became the shovel. Containers were placed at digging points and filled with soggy mud that was laden with organic material. It took countless shovels full of mud to provide the material for the road. (Courtesy of Beaufort Museum.)

The nearest thing to a mechanized, earth-moving machine the mud puppies had was the Brooks Load Lugger. The truck was similar to a dump truck in that it was used to pick up the filled containers and deliver them to where the material was needed. However, the containers could be uncoupled from the truck while being filled, and the truck could retrieve another filled container for removal to the causeway. (Courtesy of Beaufort Museum.)

Slowly the containers of mud began to mount up. The roadbeds became higher than the water at its highest point over the tidal plain. The mud dried, the earth was smoothed, and the causeway was formed. (Courtesy of Beaufort Museum.)

The larger of the two bridges built was the Harbor Island Bridge. It has a longer span due to the size of the river, and the middle section of the bridge can swing open to allow the shrimp boats which use the river as an outlet to the ocean to pass. (Courtesy of Beaufort Museum.)

Work on the Johnson Creek Bridge began at the same time as the causeway construction. Center supports were sunk to the bedrock under the river allowing for the middle of the bridge to be fabricated. When the road was completed, the bridge was then connected to the land. (Courtesy of Beaufort Museum.)

At some point in the 1940s, the causeway and bridges were complete enough to connect Beaufort and the sea islands with Hunting Island. This 16-mile road from Beaufort to the island was the beginning of a national highway. U.S. 21 would be extended along this route, and millions of people would eventually travel the road on their way to Hunting Island. (Courtesy of Beaufort Museum.)

In 1938, Beaufort was experiencing financial difficulties due to the Depression, and the park project on Hunting Island was in jeopardy. South Carolina was in the process of creating a system of parks across the state using CCC labor to build the facilities. Beaufort County agreed to transfer ownership of Hunting Island to be used as a state park, providing the state set aside 50 acres of land on the island for private use. The Department of Forestry took possession of the island and Hunting Island State Park was born. In 1993, Beaufort County sued the state to return the island to the county, claiming the provisions of the transfer had not been kept in force. (Courtesy of SC Archives and History.)

Until the causeway and bridges were completed, the CCC workers and supplies were transported to the island by boat and barge. The point of departure was generally Hilton Head, and they followed a route around Fripp Island into Johnson's Creek, so fuel restrictions did not allow for frills. The men found a spot to either sit or stand and stayed there during their journey. (Courtesy of SC Archives and History.)

When the boat landed on Hunting Island, the food and other supplies, along with the men, were unloaded and moved inland to the barracks compound. The men would usually remain on the island for the duration of their service due to the difficulty of travel. However, a weekend trip back to civilization on a supply boat was not unheard of. (Courtesy of SC Archives and History.)

The barracks located within the slash pine forest were little more than shacks. They were Spartan quarters with dormitory beds. Yet, after hours of digging, moving earth and plants, and carpentry work, they were a welcome relief to the exhausted men. (Courtesy of SC Archives and History.)

Many structures on Hunting Island State Park were built by the CCC workers. In this photograph, workers are using the same marsh mud method employed on the causeway to build a bathhouse foundation. (Courtesy of Beaufort Museum.)

This 1940 view of a parking area on the island gives an idea of how popular the state expected the park to be. This area is large enough to hold a substantial number of cars, which is surprising during a period of severe economic crisis when recreation was a luxury that few could afford. (Courtesy of SC Archives and History.)

The CCC also changed the landscape of the island. A saltwater lagoon was dredged at the southern end of the island. The lagoon was opened to the sea so that it could be affected by tide movement and allowed a large variety of ocean fish to find shelter in the gentled water. (Courtesy of SC Archives and History.)

Segregation between South Carolina's black and white citizens was the law of the land in 1940. The island was divided into separate areas and designated for use by a specific race. This portion of the beach was for whites only, and no black person dared to stray across the line. (Courtesy of Beaufort Museum.)

The Sand Dollar Interpretive Center was originally used as the black bathhouse. The center of the building then was an open breezeway with the end sections being the changing area. Later, the building was enclosed and used to for nature programs, storytelling, or just as a place to sit and watch the ocean. The building was lost to erosion in 1995.

Visitors had to bring their own provisions since there were no concession stands to provide food. Thus, another important CCC project was the clearing and establishing of picnic areas, like this one located in the "whites only" area of the forest. These picnic sites were cleared of underbrush and other obstacles, and the shaded areas provided pleasant places to eat. (Courtesy of Beaufort Museum.)

This is a photograph of the same picnic area made one month later. The facilities on the barrier island were subject to the same forces of wind and water that affected the natural environment. This would prove to be just a small lesson of what could occur to man-made areas on a barrier island. (Courtesy of Beaufort Museum.)

U.S. 21 was extended from Beaufort to Hunting Island. The highway followed the old railway bed and passed close to the lighthouse, then turned and ended along the south end of the lagoon. Beach access for day visitors was via a sandy dirt road that branched off U.S. 21 and passed to the north of the lighthouse and went directly to the beach.

Picnic and parking areas were located just off the beach inside the forest. Visitors could, until the 1970s, park next to an empty table, thus claiming it for the day. One bit of sport among frequent "day trippers" was to watch a first-time visitor become stuck in a sand bed and then assist the driver in freeing the trapped vehicle.

With the ever-present shrimp boat in the background, a surfcaster tries his luck. Fishing, either in the surf or at the lagoon, is one of the most popular activities on the island. In particular, the fall is an active time of year for anglers when the spots are running. Campers come to the island prepared to spend a week or more fishing, and they often bring freezers to store their catch.

Before erosion took its toll, there were several large beaches along the lagoon where one could park while fishing. While regular tackle was commonly used, other methods of fishing were employed. Nets could be cast to catch bait fish and an occasional shrimp. Crabbing could be done from the banks while others walked the banks to snatch for mullet.

Heavy winter storms during the late 1970s eroded the land to the point where U.S. 21 was cut between the lighthouse and lagoon. Traffic was re-routed, and the park service began to re-design the park. By the start of the 1980s, an entrance gate had been built, a network of one-way roads took visitors to various locations, the day beach had been divided into the North and South Beaches, and parking was no longer allowed on the beach.

One of the recent additions to the state park is the Garden Hammock Boardwalk. This .3-mile deck allows the visitor to walk across a salt marsh to view the various life forms that live there. The trail continues from the picnic area on the hammock across the marsh to other hammocks and ends at a wooden crabbing dock.

One of the best crabbing locations is near Russ Point at the south end of the island. Crabbing is a simple task that does not require a lot of expensive tackle. All that is needed is a length of string, a chicken neck, some lead weight, and a net. One end of the string is tied around the chicken neck, the weight is added and the other end of the string is tied to the wrist. When there is a tug on the string, the line is slowly pulled in and the crab netted.

A favored pastime among the older generations is shell collecting. Different varieties of whelks can be found on the beach, along with South Carolina's state shell, the lettered olive. Most of the shells found come from bivalve shellfish. There are only special times though when shelling is good. A high tide combined with rough waters will bring in the best shells to the shore.

One of the most popular areas on Hunting Island is the campground. This sign is located on Ladys Island at the junction of Business and Bypass U.S. 21, fourteen miles from the island. It informs the incoming camper what the chances are of getting a site. A "No Vacancy" notice means the camper will have to be very lucky to get a site.

While the campground is open all year, during the summer months, competition for a site can be very intense. The main gate opens at 6 am and there is usually a line of people waiting to get in. The campers wait in line until 8 am when the store opens, and the rangers begin to assign locations on a first-come, first-served basis. Once all the sites are rented, those remaining have to wait until the 2 pm checkout time. If no one has left by then, the remaining campers have to find another place to stay.

Once a camper has a site, he or she can remain there for up to fourteen days. There are two different sections within the campground. The first is Beachside where the sites are on or near the beach. Across the road from the store is Mosquito Alley, which is in the maritime forest. Stagnant water acts as breeding ground for the little pests, and campers are constantly searching for effective repellents.

Beach erosion has done considerable damage to the campground in the 1990s. Until 1995, there were two hundred sites available for rental. Twelve "Beachside" locations were washed away, leaving only exposed electrical cable and broken pavement. New sites are being built to replace those which have been lost, but they are all being put in "Mosquito Alley."

The main attraction at Hunting Island State Park is the 4-mile beach. The beach is open all year, with nearly five thousand people per day using the shore during the summer months.

A number of amateur shutterbugs constantly prowl the ever-changing beach in search of photographs. Most of these images are put in family photo albums as vacation memories, while others are hung on walls as decoration. Since the State Park Commission doesn't have a policy of visually recording events on the island, the amateur photographers play an important role in remembering the island by keeping a photographic record.

The shallow waters caused by the shallow sloping of the continental shelf do not make for good surfing conditions. Yet, when storms and other conditions increase the size of the waves, there will be someone on the island looking for the perfect ride. The deterioration of the beach in the 1990s has made the sport less popular here.

Before the park service placed restrictions on the activity, sitting on the dunes was popular with the younger generations, whether it was a young couple who were trying to make their relationship stronger or, like this girl, someone finding a good place to study. The ridge of a primary dune was a perfect place to watch people on the beach and view the ocean.

The most popular thing to do on the beach is simply walk the line between the ocean and shore. The hot sand is cooled by the water so one can be barefoot, and a bathing suit is the uniform of the day. Walking can be a wonderful activity for the body and the spirit. Many health-conscious people use the 4 miles of sea frontage in the early morning or late afternoon for aerobic exercise. Others simply like to show off what genetics and a vigorous exercise routine have brought about. The absence of bustling crowds and carnival-like attractions allows the walker to contemplate the mysteries of the universe or what to have for dinner. The beach brings a calming peace in a world of chaos.

A relaxing activity that can be done on the beach is sunbathing. There are numerous places where a person can spread a blanket on the ground and enjoy the sun. Though the medical community has cautioned against such exposure to the sun, the desire for browned skin causes many people to ignore these warnings.

Some people utilize the beach to do absolutely nothing. A cool drink, a shaded area, and a good friend are all that is required to make a pleasant afternoon.

The most recognizable landmark on Hunting Island is the lighthouse. As this drawing from 1874 shows, its major function was to act as a navigational aid for ships. The first lighthouse was built in 1859 and destroyed by Confederate troops during the War Between the States. The second tower was completed in 1875. The lighthouse was moved in 1889 to its present location because of the problems of erosion on the beachfront. (Courtesy National Archives.)

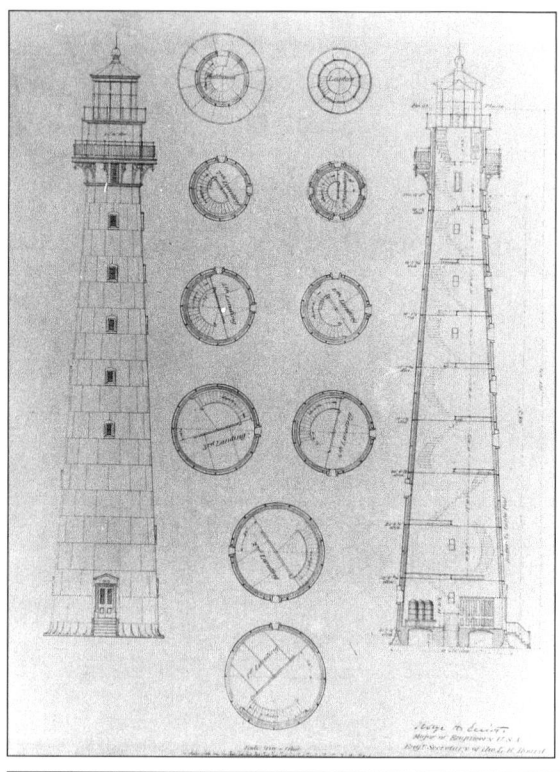

This drawing features the construction of the 1875 lighthouse. Classified as a second order beacon, the structure stands 133 feet above the mean high tide. The only permanent residents on the island were the lighthouse keepers and their families. The lighthouse was taken out of service in 1933 and the compound deeded to Beaufort County. (Courtesy National Archives.)

Access to the beacon housing was by walking up a spiral, metal staircase. The bottom step at the entrance of the lighthouse is the first of 185 steps which lead to the beacon room. Visitors today can follow the staircase only to the observation deck just outside the glass housing.

The small white building to the side of the lighthouse was used for oil storage. The flame for the beacon was provided by burning vaporized oil inside a hollow wick. The paint design on the lighthouse was its signature. Each of the 256 national lighthouses had a unique paint pattern, along with a specific flashing sequence so when a ship's captain saw a light, he would know his location and the dangers he faced.

The lighthouse compound consisted of the lighthouse, oil storage building, the keeper's house, several storage buildings, and two cisterns. The staff consisted of a keeper and two assistant keepers. The ultimate responsibility of the keepers was to maintain the beacon, even under the most adverse conditions. A local resident states that the keeper's house burned in 1938 when a group of men playing cards in the house accidentally knocked over a lantern. (Courtesy of SC Archives and History.)

This photograph, made from the observation deck of the lighthouse in 1938, shows how far the structure was from the sea. One of the island's inland fresh water lagoons is visible along with a well-defined dune system and maritime forest. (Courtesy of SC Archives and History.)

When the second lighthouse was built, its location was criticized because some felt its quarter-mile distance from the ocean was too far. By 1889, it had to be moved to its present location to save it from the ocean. This photograph, made in the 1990s, shows how much erosion has occurred since 1938. The ocean is now less than 100 yards from the compound and again is a threat to the lighthouse.(Courtesy of Amanda Cole.)

The remoteness of the island meant that supplies of beacon oil, food, and other items had to be brought to the island by boat. The supply boats would leave the depot on Hilton Head and travel around the northern end of Hunting Island to Johnson's Creek. A wharf was located on Johnson's Creek where the provisions could be unloaded. (Courtesy of SC Archives and History.)

A narrow gauge railroad, similar to the one in this photograph, was used to transport the supplies overland from the wharf to the compound. Old U.S. 21 followed the railbed's path through the maritime forest as it wound its way to the lagoon. The remnants of the dock and walkway are still visible in the marsh. (Courtesy of SC Archives and History.)

Hunting Island was not considered a desirable duty station due to its remote location. The island was uninhabited except for the keepers. Alligators and poisonous snakes could create life-threatening situations. Usually, the only visitor to the island was the lighthouse inspector who called at Hunting Island once every three months. The isolated residents had to be self-sufficient by raising gardens and hunting wild game.

Despite the dense forest and underbrush, the lack of roadways and swamps, mosquitoes and malaria, and fierce animals, the keepers of the light did their job of keeping that light burning. In 1933, the federal government put out the light.

Five
The Wildlife Sanctuary

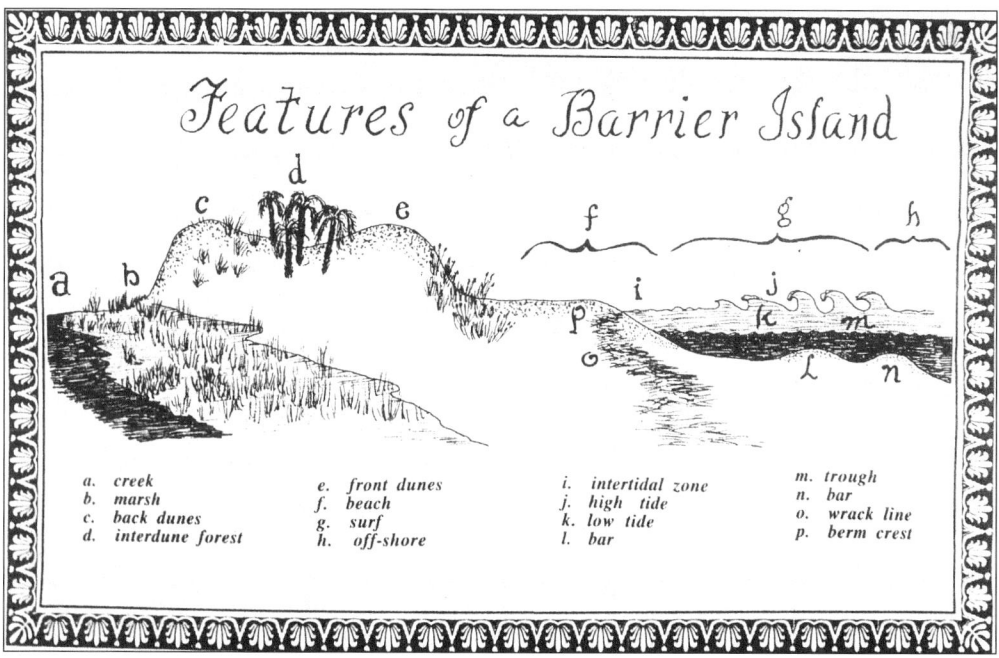

Features of a Barrier Island

a. creek
b. marsh
c. back dunes
d. interdune forest
e. front dunes
f. beach
g. surf
h. off-shore
i. intertidal zone
j. high tide
k. low tide
l. bar
m. trough
n. bar
o. wrack line
p. berm crest

The barrier islands of South Carolina are over four thousand years old. They differ significantly from the sea islands which were once a part of the mainland and are built on the same bedrock. Barrier islands were formed by the buildup of sediments brought from the Appalachian Mountains as the rivers flowed to the sea. As the island grew seaward, new dunes were built in front of older dunes, making rows of protective barriers against the ocean. In these protected zones, plant and land animal life could thrive. A mature barrier island has a unique profile, and each area has its own function to perform. (Courtesy of the collection of Jerry Morris.)

Building from the ocean, the beach is the first important area on a barrier island. At low tide, the beach is one of the most severe and dangerous environments for life. Salt spray, constant high temperatures, the desiccation caused by the sun, and the action of the surf all combine to prevent plant life from surviving on the open beach. Animals can protect themselves by burrowing into the sand or finding protected areas while they await the return of high tide. Anything that lives on the beach is at the mercy of the ocean, for there is very little protection from the wind and water.

Sand dunes are an important feature in the construction of a barrier island. Dune construction is greatest during the summer months when the winds and water are calmer. Sand is distributed across the beach by the wind until it is deposited against some obstacle. The dunes are fundamental to protecting the maritime forest and salt marsh from flooding by the surf and severe storms which blow in from the ocean. Due to a high erosion rate, there are few natural sand dunes remaining on Hunting Island except at the northern end of the island. Marine Corps bulldozers spent the beginning months of 1997 pushing up sand at South Beach to form new dunes in order to replace those lost to storms.

Sea oats are a special type of grass which help protect the sand dunes. It is one of the a very few plants which is salt tolerant and resistant to the severe beach conditions, thus making it able to survive along and on a dune line. Its tap roots penetrate several feet into the ground in search of water, and the leaves at the base form a bush-like structure which catches and holds sand.

Sea oats are found in the more hostile environment of the primary dunes which are closest to salt water. Seeds from the plants are carried by the wind and deposited along the dune line to start new colonies. Because of the importance of the sea oats to the building and stabilization of sand dunes, the plant is under federal protection.

The primary dunes are almost totally gone at the center of Hunting Island, and there are very few secondary dunes remaining. The sea oats have migrated inland to what is left of the secondary dune line and maritime forest and are replacing the less salt-tolerant plants, such as wax myrtle and live oaks.

The maritime forest is located in the interior of Hunting Island behind the dunes. It is one of the few undisturbed forests left in South Carolina. The forest contains a great diversity of bush plants and trees. These plants are not salt tolerant and must be protected from salt spray by the dunes. The trees, especially the hardwoods, provide life support for migrating birds in the spring and fall. Birds can find a wide variety of insects on which to feed, along with fruit from the wax myrtle, palmetto, magnolia, and holly. The maritime forest has been subject to damage from strong storms, fires, and erosion to the point where there are few large trees left on the island.

Hunting Island has one of the best developed slash pine forests in South Carolina. The high percentage of these and other evergreen trees are helpful to the existence of the forest. Their shedding of leaves throughout the year add nutrients to the sandy soil.

The cabbage palmetto is South Carolina's state tree. Its importance to the state is demonstrated by its placement on the state flag and seal. The tree was used by Colonial troops during the American Revolution on Sullivan's Island to build fortifications. The soft, springy wood repelled the shells from the British fleet and helped bring about a Colonial victory.

Much of the land in the maritime forest is low lying and swampy. When the spring rains arrive, stagnant water collects in these areas. These swamps become breeding grounds for mosquitoes. Though malaria, a mosquito-borne disease, is no longer a major problem, the pests can make human life very uncomfortable during the spring and summer.

Directly opposite the beach and protected by both the sand dunes and maritime forest is the tidal salt marsh. This sea of cord grass is home to a large group of sea and land creatures. The marsh provides food for these animals in the form of organic material from the grasses, algae, and bacteria. The two zones, high and low, in the salt marsh are breeding grounds and nurseries for many of of the marine animals that are important to the coastal economy. Shrimp, crabs, and game fish spend the first part of their lives in this rich "soup" until they are ready to enter the open ocean.

Life in the saltwater marsh is governed by the ocean's tides. High tide causes a flurry of activity all along the food chain that is hidden just beneath the water's surface. At low tide, the marsh flats seemingly come alive with fiddler and marsh crabs, along with raccoons, as they search the land surface for food.

Oysters thrive in the marshes and contribute to the marsh's survival. The bivalves attach themselves to stationary objects and feed by filtering water through their gills and other cilia. At the same time, they clean contaminants that pass through the salt marsh from the water. In many estuaries along the South Carolina coast, oystering is not allowed due to the level of water pollution.

Hammocks are areas of elevated ground found in a marsh which are not covered by water during high tide. This photograph shows the birth of a hammock. At some point in time, a tree seed landed in a spot with the proper amount of salinity and nutrients to allow it to germinate. As the tree grew, it periodically shed some of its leaves which, along with other detritus, formed a compost that nourished the tree and raised the level of the earth. Then small, bushy plants began to take root in the raised earth. The hammock will not extend beyond the drip line of the tree until enough detritus and sediment have been trapped by the plants to enlarge the small island.

A wide variety of animals use Hunting Island for some purpose. During the summer, loggerhead turtles use the beaches as a nesting ground for their eggs. The turtles come ashore at night and dig a hole in the sand with their flippers. They then lay an average of 125 eggs, cover the nest, and return to the sea. Loggerhead turtles are listed as an endangered species, so the park service monitors turtle activity on the island. The beach is patrolled every morning during the season by volunteers. When a nest is found and it appears to be in danger of being affected by erosion or saltwater, experienced personnel relocate the eggs to a hatchery cage. The wire cage also provides protection from predators like raccoons. After about sixty days, the hatchlings emerge and make a rush for the ocean. It is estimated that predators and pollution will claim the majority of the turtles so that only four out of every thousand become adults.

The Atlantic Blue Crab can be found in abundance in the creeks and marshes on Hunting Island. The blue crab is an important commercial crustacean to the United States fishing economy. One of the most popular forms of the crab is the soft shell or "buster." When the crab molts, it take several hours for the new shell to harden. While the shell is soft, the crab can be cleaned, fried, and eaten in its entirety. Lump crab meat which is taken from under the carapace is used in stews or to prepare deviled crab. The front claws, or pincers, can deliver a painful wound, as many a casual surf walker has found.

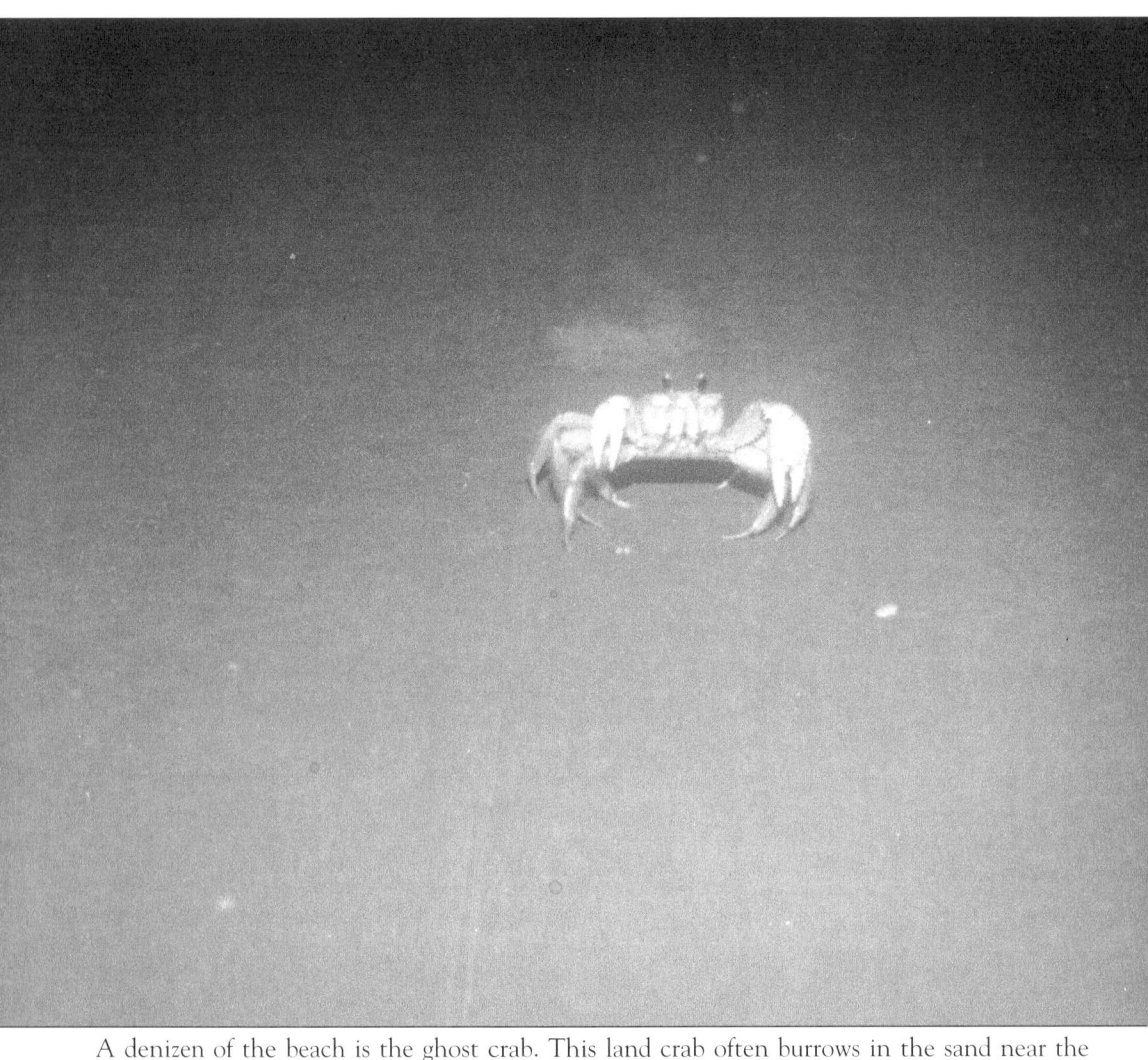

A denizen of the beach is the ghost crab. This land crab often burrows in the sand near the dunes above the high tide line. Though more active at night, it can be found roaming the beach near the entrance of its burrow during the day. The crab is named for its sand-colored shell that helps camouflage it from birds.

There are approximately 140 different species of birds which live permanently on or migrate through Hunting Island. The most common bird found on the beach is the seagull. These opportunistic scavengers are constantly searching for food, such as dead sea creatures washed up on the beach or fish cast aside by fishermen. These birds will eat anything, including cold, leftover, fast-food fries.

Common land animals can be found in the maritime forest. One of the most active is the gray squirrel. This member of the rodent family hunts for food on the ground, then retreats to the tree to feed. The presence of humans on the island has altered the squirrel's feeding habits, turning it into a scavenger. When careless visitors leave food unattended, a squirrel will take advantage of a free meal.

Another scavenger that lives in the maritime forest and salt marshes is the raccoon. This little thief became a major problem in the campground. The raccoons became adept at opening ice chests, refrigerators, and any other container that wasn't locked. Campers would be awakened at night by the sound of raccoons rummaging in food containers. The movement of trash bins to other areas, along with a major raccoon relocation program, has helped to reduce the problem.

The Hunting Island deer is what originally brought the planters to the island. The deer and other small game provided meat for their diet. After the War Between the States, the island was a hunter's paradise for rich Northern businessmen, who took deer in large quantities on their hunting trips. One of the owners of the island in the 1920s was Dr. Arthur Elting, who was associated with the railroads that brought hunters to Beaufort County. (Courtesy of Beaufort Museum.)

This unique subspecies of white-tailed deer can only be found on Hunting Island and several nearby barrier islands. They are usually seen during the early morning or evening hours in the forested areas, though their tracks and spoor can be found on the beach. Due to a lack of hunting pressure, these deer have lost most of their fear of humans to the point that visitors illegally feed them by hand.

One of Hunting Island's more elegant birds is the snowy egret. It is a wading bird which is most frequently found fishing for food in the salt marsh. It almost became extinct because of the value of its plumage used for women's hats, but protection has allowed it to make a recovery.

Alligators thrive on Hunting Island, though they are reclusive reptiles. They are generally found at the Visitor's Center pond and the lagoon. Extreme care should be taken when one encounters an alligator, for the reptile is carnivorous and can be very aggressive. While there are no known attack incidents on the island, alligators have attacked and killed people in South Carolina waters. There is a recorded account of an alligator that got inside the lighthouse compound and threatened the keeper's wife.

Flying in a perfect fighter formation, the brown pelican appears to be the aerial protector of Hunting Island. They fly in from the north over the forest and then bank out over the ocean to soar only a few feet above the ocean waves. When food is spotted, the pelican will fold its wings to its body and dive into the water. The pelican is another bird which was threatened with extinction because of human pollution. Pesticides, such as DDT, entered their food chain and made the shells of their eggs very thin. The eggs would break under the weight of the bird in the nest. Federal protection and the removal of the destructive chemicals from the environment have allowed the birds to recover.

Six
A Vanishing Paradise

Barrier islands are important to South Carolina's coast. They are the front line of defense against wind, waves, and storms for the forests and salt marshes. A barrier island is in a constant state of flux, always reshaping and rebuilding itself. Hunting Island has the highest average rate of beach erosion of the South Carolina islands at 15 feet per year. There are many factors which cause the loss of beach sand, but the main features are the location and size of the shoals, wave alignment to the beach, and water currents. As waves reach the beach, they break to the north and south, taking sand with them. Before the sand can be redeposited on the island, strong inlet currents from St. Helena Sound and Fripp Inlet sweep away the sand to other locations. (Courtesy of the collection of Melinda Smyre.)

Problems with erosion are not a recent event on Hunting Island. This photograph made in 1938 shows the effects of severe winter storms. During a three-week period from October 27th to November 19th, Hunting Island lost 22 feet of beach. (Courtesy of SC Archives and History.)

This photograph graphically illustrates how much sand was lost during the 1938 storms. The 22 feet of lost beach was a linear measurement and did not take in account the depth of the sand. Most of the sand lost from the primary dunes had depths deeper than an average man's height. (Courtesy of SC Archives and History.)

Following the storms, the beach was littered with the debris of up-rooted trees and brush. As this debris dried, it posed a fire hazard to the island. It lay like giant piles of firewood, and a lightning strike from a summer storm could trigger a major forest fire. (Courtesy of SC Archives and History.)

Damage to the maritime forest didn't end when the storms were over. Tree root systems were weakened by the removal of the sand, allowing trees to be blown over more easily when the next storm hit. Also, the trees were not salt tolerant, and salt spray blown from the ocean on the tree roots greatly reduced the trees' chances for survival. (Courtesy of SC Archives and History.)

The summer storms which hit Hunting Island are usually very intense. Low pressure centers are generated in warm tropical waters and their strength is intensified by the heat of the sun. They can vary in size from a minor squall to a major hurricane. This photograph is of the feeder bands of Tropical Depression Alfredo as it passed near Hunting Island. The storm gave the island a glancing blow and put on a spectacular display of cloud formations, but it flooded the city of Atlanta under many inches of rain.

The hurricane which hit Beaufort in 1893 is considered to be the largest storm to have made landfall in the area during recorded history. Only estimates can be made of its strength since there were no recording devices available. This view of Bay Street shows the amount of damage done. Trees uprooted, buildings turned into piles of broken lumber, and human death and injury were the legacy of the hurricane. (Courtesy of Beaufort County Library.)

This NOAA satellite photo is from the 1996 hurricane season showing Hurricane Fran as it neared Beaufort. At first, its path was calculated to make landfall in Beaufort, but it changed course and destroyed Topsail Beach in North Carolina. It is never a matter of *if* a hurricane will hit a coastal area, but rather, *when*. The last hurricane to visit Hunting Island was Gracie in 1959. Since then, the populace has conveniently forgotten what such a storm can do.

While hurricanes can generate large-scale damage from high winds and tidal surges, their presence in a coastal area is very short. The most intense beach destruction results from winter storms called nor'easters. These low pressure systems form offshore, sometimes several in rapid succession, and can stall off a coastal location and lash the shore for days.

Nor'easters are so named because their winds come from the northeast. While they don't have the heat of the sun and travel time over open waters to build wind speed, they can still generate hurricane-force winds. The wind increases the wave rate, and whitecaps form on the ocean. When the waves break on the shore, the gale blows salt spray from the tops of the waves. This spray affects trees and plants by creating a shearing effect that prunes the plants.

Meteorologists try to calculate at what tide a hurricane will make landfall to assess the probable damage. The higher the tide, the more destruction the storm surge will make. The time a nor'easter arrives is not as important because the duration of the storm at a given point will usually encompass both high and low tides. The problems from nor'easters arise at high tide when water is forced through low points in the dunes and flood the maritime forest.

Like snow being blown in a blizzard, sand is driven by the wind across the beach. Tons of sand are relocated during a nor'easter. This sand is taken from the dry areas in front of and on the dunes. This reduces the size of the primary dune and inhibits its ability to protect the forests and marshes.

A portion of the wind-driven sand is trapped by the fibrous roots of a cabbage palmetto. The "shadow effect" on the underlying earth can be seen as sand is trapped on the opposite side of the tree. The top dressing of protective sand has been stripped away, leaving the substrata bare.

As the water is whipped into foam and precious sand is removed, the roots of a tree are exposed. The threats to the tree from lack of support and salt exposure are the prime causes of tree loss in the maritime forest. During the winter of 1996/97, over a hundred pines trees had to be cut because of saltwater flooding.

Trees blown down by the winds can make the beach appear like a war zone. Downed trees litter the beach, along with the exposed stumps of other trees which succumbed to earlier nor'easters.

The destruction left behind from a nor'easter can remain for months. Other trees are left unstable and can fall over from their own weight. These trees are generally cut to remove the danger of one unexpectedly falling on a visitor. The trees will be left where they have fallen or will be collected into a pile on the beach to form barriers around which new sand dunes can form.

The works of man are not exempt from the forces of a nor'easter. These pieces of pavement are the only remains of a road which was washed away by the storm. The winter of 1996/97 saw the loss of two private cabins on the southern end of the island and a public bathhouse at North Beach.

A nor'easter will deposit tree limbs, marsh straw, and other debris on the shore. The line of sea straw left by the high tide marks how far the seawater came on the beach. This photograph shows that only a few feet separate a small line of dunes and the highest rise of the salt water.

The Park Service is making every effort to reduce the amount of erosion on Hunting Island. One method that is used is the building of drift fences. The wooden slats collect wind-blown sand, while the air spaces permit the wind to pass through without damaging the fence. Five beach replenishment efforts have also been done since 1968, but these methods are like putting a bandage on a slashed artery. The new dunes can be erased in a few hours by a nor'easter or extreme high tides.

A jetty is a structure built perpendicular to the shore that traps moving sand. This jetty at the Point on the northern end of the island is a micro-view of both the negative and positive aspects of human intervention in the erosion problem. As the longshore transport moves the sand along the beach, the intrusion of the jetty is causing the area to the north of the wall to accrete while the area to the south is being deprived of sand. As larger projects are undertaken on other barrier islands to protect expensive residential property, the positive and negative effects of those projects will impact the erosion rates on other barrier islands, often in undesirable ways.

While erosion is thought to occur only on the beach, the island's lagoon has suffered the effects of depletion. The broad beach is now gone and the trees that line the shore are being undercut by the water and are falling into the lake. The dissipation of the sand dunes along South Beach has created a situation which could alter the island's future topography. If a category three or greater hurricane hits the island, the conditions are right for a new inlet to be cut from South Beach to the lagoon, thus creating a new, smaller island

A biblical parable warned of the dangers of building a house on sand. While natural forces have an important part in the erosion of Hunting Island, human factors which affect land shift have to be taken into consideration. Sand to replenish the beach is no longer being deposited on the shore because the rivers that carry it from the mountains have been dammed to provide electricity. Land developers use methods to build their beach frontage to the disadvantage of the other barrier islands along the coast. In the final analysis, the natural forces of the coastal system will be the final arbitrator of island ownership. A deed is a very flimsy shield against the power of wind and water. A person who builds a permanent dwelling on land that is constantly changing and re-forming will find himself or herself the willing victim of society's greed.

This "fallen hero" is symbolic of the changes that have and continue to happen on Hunting Island. Twenty-five years ago, one could expect to notice only minor alterations to the land during a visit. In 1996, the revisions appear to have accelerated to an alarming rate. Old friends such as the Sand Dollar are gone, the walk from the lighthouse to the beach is much shorter, and the shoals at the Point appear to be growing larger. Yet, those who have a true affection for the island appear to be ignoring what is happening and continue to implement plans developed for a park which existed in years past but is now being rapidly altered.

There are some things that will never change on Hunting Island. The sun will continue to rise in the east and, as long as the island remains a state park, the sea breezes will be free for all to feel. Waves that had their birth in Africa continue to break on an island thousands of miles away. The heat, the humidity, and the mosquitoes will always be present to make us value the simple pleasures that a breezy beach has to offer. Porpoises frolic offshore while the shrimpers fling wide their nets. Hunting Island is still a place of peace, of solace, and of regeneration for the body and the spirit.